Forewords

From Peter

The idea for this recipe book came during a dinner party at Beena's house a couple of years ago. An invitation to a dinner cooked by Beena is an event not to be missed, and during the inevitable compliments from all the guests during the meal, her husband Peter remarked that all these recipes were prepared from memory and should be written down for the benefit in particular of family and friends. She has memorised dozens of South Indian recipes, so I volunteered to write them up while at the same time being taught how to cook Indian food.   I have tried to set out the process in the sort of easy steps that should enable anyone to follow them – even someone like myself with absolutely no experience of cooking anything.

Beena was born in Kerala, in the South of India, and lived in Southern India for the next 30 years, during which time she learned all about the traditional ways of cooking from her mother, aunts and other relatives. In many respects dishes from Southern India are quite different from the meals we are used to seeing in Indian restaurants in the UK, most of which are influenced by the dishes of the Northern part of the sub-continent.

Before our first lesson, Beena took me to an Asian supermarket to buy the spices. Although most of the spices are available from the bigger UK supermarket chains, those from the Asian stores are usually cheaper, and the variety more comprehensive. A list of the spices and other standard ingredients is included.

Oct.2010

From Beena
There is the involvement of two Peters here, mine and Evelyn's.
For the sake of distinction, Peter Aitken will henceforth be known
to me as Peter the Shishya (Indian term for apprentice/pupil).

Peter the Shishya has been an ideal student. He practised all the
recipes between sessions (on average 3 dishes per session) and
he entertained his friends to delicious meals.
His note keeping was excellent and this book would not be in
existence but for his efforts.

Oct 2010

Acknowledgements

We would like to thank all those who contributed to the
production of this book in a direct or indirect way.
We thank all those friends who trialled some of the recipes.
Our special thanks to Caroline, James, Nicholas, Santosh and
Vijay, our reliable food critics.
We thank Peter for his ideas, technical support and
encouragement and Evelyn for her unwavering support and
being there for Peter A, always.

Cooking terms and general tips

- ➤ Where there is a reference in the recipe to oil, this refers to vegetable oil of any variety or cost.
- ➤ If you are tempted to experiment and invent a recipe of your own, a standard mixture of spices that you will find useful is: - 4 parts coriander powder, to 2 parts cumin powder, to 1 part chilli powder, to ½ part powdered turmeric.
- ➤ Ginger and garlic in equal proportions, chopped then crushed finely, can be frozen in units of one tablespoonful. You can then use the frozen mixture next time the recipe calls for it, this saving a lot of time on the day.
- ➤ Bursting mustard seeds. Heat oil to a high temperature then add the mustard seeds. Cover immediately as they will cause hot oil to spit up from the pan. They will burst in a minute or so.
- ➤ Dry roasting. Heat a frying pan to a high temperature but add no oil or water. Add the seeds to be roasted, keep stirring until they begin to brown.
- ➤ Ventilation. Ensure adequate ventilation when bursting mustard seeds or frying chillies.
- ➤ Crushing and powdering. It is useful to have a mortar and pestle for this process.
- ➤ Making coconut milk. Dissolve 25g creamed coconut in 50ml of very hot water.
- ➤ Pungency. For making the food very hot add more chillies. For milder food reduce the amount of chillies.

Keys

tsp = a level tea spoon
dsp = a level dessert spoon
tbsp= a level table spoon

ml = millilitre

Spices and other necessary ingredients

Black eye beans
Red lentils
Ground turmeric
Chilli powder
Curry powder
Ground coriander
Poppy seeds(white)
Ground ginger
Ground cumin
Cumin whole
Mung beans
Garam masala
Black cardamom pods
Whole black pepper
Whole cloves
Whole nutmeg
Elaichi (cardamom)
Mustard seeds
Whole coriander seeds

Whole coriander seeds
Kala jeera
Cinnamon sticks
Tamarind
Coconut milk
Chick peas
Tomato puree
Chunky chat masala
Sambar masala
Fenugreek seeds
Dried chillies
Curry leaves
Desiccated coconut
Tofu
Compounded asafoetida
Breadcrumbs
Whole fennel seeds
Pure butter ghee

Contents

FIRST COURSES

Sweet and Sour Potato

Serves 4

2 sweet potatoes
1 dsp oil
2 spring onions, finely chopped
1 large green chilli deseeded and finely chopped
3 tbsp of white wine vinegar
2 heaped dsp of liquid honey
¼ tsp of salt

Scrub the sweet potatoes but leave the skins on.
Cut in half lengthwise.
Place on a baking tray, drizzle the oil over them and cook in a
preheated oven at 200*C for 40 to 45 minutes (i.e. until soft.)
Mix in a bowl the honey, onion, chilli and vinegar.
This becomes the dressing to be poured over the potatoes.
Serve straight from the oven.

Onion Bhaji

Serves 8

100g gram flour
½ tsp curry powder
¼ tsp chilli powder
½ tsp baking powder
¼ tsp salt
1 onion coarsely chopped
Vegetable oil for deep frying
100ml water

Sieve the flour, curry powder, chilli powder, baking powder and salt into a bowl.
Mix in the water to make a smooth batter.
Mix the onion with the batter.

Heat an inch depth of oil in a large saucepan.
Get oil very hot.
Put a dozen spoonfuls of the mixture into the oil.
Fry for 4 minutes turning over once.
Use moderate heat until golden.
Transfer to a colander lined with kitchen roll to absorb oil.

Note: The batter may be used to make bhaji with sliced potato/cauliflower florets/sliced aubergine

Mint Chutney
Serves 4-6

30g fresh mint
½ green chilli
4 tbsp plain yoghurt and a little water
Juice of half a lime
½ tsp salt

Put all the ingredients through a blender and use as a dip for the bhaji.

Kovalam Fish Cutlets

Serves 10-12 (starter) 6-8 (main)

2 medium mashed potatoes (about 150g)
500g of cheap fish
220g smoked mackerel
1 medium chilli coarsely chopped
½ inch root ginger finely chopped
1 medium onion finely chopped
1 tsp curry powder
1 tsp fennel seeds
Vegetable oil
1 egg
Dry breadcrumbs

Place the fish in a 2 litre bowl, sprinkle with water and microwave
on full power for 4 minutes.
Drain water from fish. Remove skin and bone and flake when
cool enough to handle.
Skin the mackerel and flake into small pieces.
Mix both lots of fish with the potato.
Dry roast fennel seeds for 2 minutes. Crush in a mortar and
 add to the fish mixture.
Heat 1 tbsp oil and cook the onion, chilli and ginger until the
onion is translucent.
Add curry powder and cook for 5 minutes on a low heat.
Add this mixture and the fennel to the fish and let it cool.
Squeeze the mix by hand to ensure thorough mixing.
Form golf ball sized balls with the mixture and then flatten into
fish cakes.

Beat the egg, dip each fishcake in it and then coat with
breadcrumbs.

For frying, heat 2 tbsp oil on full heat. Reduce heat to half and
place fishcakes in to fry for 5 minutes on each side.
Shallow fry them in batches of 6.

Pesarutu

Serves 6

150g mung beans.
½ onion
1 small chilli
1 tbsp rice
½ tsp salt
½ inch root ginger

Soak rice and beans for 10 minutes.
Put all ingredients in the blender with ¾ cup of water and the salt.
Wipe the inside of a small frying pan with oil and spread mixture one tablespoonful at a time to form pancakes. Fry for two minutes.
Serve with coconut chutney (see next).

Coconut chutney

Serves 4-6

3 tbsp desiccated coconut*
1 medium sized chilli*
1 tbsp chopped coriander leaves*
1 slice of root ginger*
Juice of half a lime*
½ tsp salt*

1 small onion, coarsely chopped[#]
½ tsp mustard seeds[#]
1 tbsp oil[#]
½ tsp urad dhal (optional) [#]

* For the chutney
[#] For the seasoning

Soak coconut in hot water for 5 minutes.
Then place the chutney ingredients in the blender and grind to a smooth mixture.

Heat the oil in a frying pan.
Burst mustard seeds in the hot oil.
Add the onion and urad dhal and cook continuously stirring until the onion starts to caramelise.
Add the coconut mixture and heat until the mixture is warm.
This can be served cold or warm.

Spicy Ladies Fingers

Serves 4

200 g okra
½ tsp turmeric
½ tsp chilli powder
1 tsp cumin powder
1 tsp garam masala
1/10th tsp salt
Oil

Wipe the okra with kitchen roll and slit along the length to within half an inch of the ends.
Mix the remaining ingredients.
Fill the slits with the above mixture and shallow fry for 5 minutes.
Ensure you turn the okra over to enable even cooking.
This can be used as a starter or a side dish.
 If as a starter, 2 per person will be adequate.

Cucumber Salad

Serves 4

1 medium cucumber in 1/8" slices
1 tsp salt
10ml white wine vinegar
A pinch of chilli flakes

Place the sliced cucumber in a colander and sprinkle with the salt.
Stand for ¼ hour then dry with clean tea towel or kitchen roll.
Arrange on a long flat dish in overlapping format.
Sprinkle the chilli flakes into the vinegar and pour it over the cucumber.

Magnolia Duck

Serves 6

200g sliced duck in ½" slivers
1 tsp soy sauce *
1 tsp Worcester sauce *
1 heaped tsp garam masala *
½ medium onion, finely chopped
1 tbsp oil
1 tbsp cumin powder
Another ½ tsp garam masala
¼ tsp salt

1 Orange #
½ medium onion, sliced lengthwise #
2 tbsp vinegar #
1 tsp red peppercorns #

A number of chapattis – 2 per diner is usual.

* For the marinade.   # For the relish.

Duck
Place the duck in the marinade for at least one hour.
Heat the oil and cook onion on a high heat for one minute then add the cumin powder and the garam masala.
Remove from heat and add the duck, mix.
Return to high heat and stir rapidly. Add salt and cook for 2 minutes.

Relish
Steep the onion in vinegar.
Cut rind from the orange and slice the flesh into inch chunks.
Add the peppercorns to the orange in a bowl.
Drain vinegar from the onion and add onion to the orange and serve.
Diners will roll up some duck and some relish in a chapatti.

Chapatti and Prawns

Serves 6

For Chapatti
400g chapatti flour
½ tsp salt
300ml warm water (approx)

For Prawn curry
2 peppers (any colour)
1 tbsp ginger-garlic paste
4 tomatoes in small pieces
2tbsp tomato puree
1 medium onion, finely chopped
425g raw uncooked peeled prawns
1 small green chilli, coarsely chopped
2 tbsp curry powder
2 tbsp coriander powder
1 dessert spoon honey
1 dessert spoon soy sauce
2 tbsp oil
Fresh coriander for garnish
100g coconut milk

Chapatti
Sieve the flour and salt and into a two 2 litre bowl. Make a well in the middle, add the water and mix.
Knead the mixture to form a soft dough.
Cover with a damp cloth and leave in fridge for one to two hours.
Form into half tennis ball sized spheres and roll out to tea plate size circles. Heat a large frying pan (high heat – no oil) – place dough in the pan.
The chapatti should be kept moving around the pan for one minute, turning a couple of times.
Smear with butter and serve.

Prawn curry

Cut peppers to inch cubes.
Heat oil and add onion and cook until translucent.
Add ginger-garlic paste and the chilli and fry for 30 seconds.
Add the curry powder and coriander powder to the pan and stir over a medium heat for 5 minutes, then add the peppers and tomatoes/tomato puree.
Cover and cook for 5 minutes.
Add soy sauce, coconut milk and honey and stir.
Add 80ml of water. Cover and cook on low to medium heat for 50 minutes until the oil separates out.
Add the prawns, stir and leave to cook for 5 minutes before serving.
(When using an electric cooker, turn the heat off after adding the prawns, cover and leave on the ring for 5 minutes.)

Red Fish Curry with Tapioca

Serves 8

900g tapioca (cassava), frozen
4 mackerels
2 tbsp oil
1 medium onion, finely chopped
2 tbsp coriander powder
1 tbsp cumin powder
1 tsp curry powder
1 tsp chilli powder
140g double concentration tomato puree
400ml water
1 tsp tamarind pulp
½ tsp salt

Tapioca
Boil tapioca in a large pan until soft – this takes about 20 to 30 minutes.

Fish
Cut the mackerel into quarters.
Chop onion finely.
Heat the oil in a pan on medium heat, add onion and cook until translucent. Add coriander, cumin and curry powder. Then add the tomato puree, chilli powder and stir the mixture.
Next add water and salt and cook for two minutes on low heat.
Mix tamarind with 100ml of water, add to the mixture and stir well.
Cook for 2 minutes then place the fish in the sauce and cook until the oil begins to separate out – about 30 minutes.
Strain the tapioca.
Serve with the fish and sauce.

Vegetable cutlet

Serves 10

250g carrots in ¼ inch cubes
250g fine green beans in ¼ inch pieces
200g peas
500g potatoes
2"piece root ginger finely chopped
1 ½ large green chillies coarsely chopped
1 tsp garam masala
1 tbsp oil
3 tbsp fresh coriander coarsely chopped
1 tsp ground black pepper
1 ½ tsp salt
2 eggs
Breadcrumbs
2 medium sized onions finely chopped
Mango chutney

Boil and mash the potatoes.
Boil beans, peas and carrots for 2 minutes then drain and dry them thoroughly.
Heat oil in pan and cook the onion until translucent; reduce heat.
Add garam masala, ginger and chilli and cook for 5 minutes then place them in a large bowl with the potato, carrots, coriander, pepper, salt, beans and peas, mix and leave in the fridge for at least half an hour.
Beat the eggs.
Remove the mixture from the fridge and form into golf ball sized quantities then flatten to oval shapes.
Dip in the beaten egg and coat with breadcrumbs.
Shallow fry for 2 minutes each side in hot oil.
Serve with the mango chutney

Spiced carrot

Serves 4

1 medium onion
4 cloves of garlic
1 large green chilli
2 inches of root ginger
- all finely chopped

2 tbsp vegetable oil
2 tsp garam masala
1 large carrot (175g) in ¼" strips of length 3-4 inches
Salt

Fry the onion and garlic until translucent.
Add the garam masala and mix then add the carrot, chilli, ginger and salt.
Stir well, add 3 tablespoonfuls of water, then cover and cook for 10 minutes.

MAIN COURSES

Scribe's Chops

Serves 6 to 8

This recipe has come down from Beena's maternal great grand parents home. Her great grand father was known as Mathai- writer because he was a scribe by profession.
Incidentally, Peter the Shishya has been Beena's scribe.

1kg of lamb, without bone or fat, cut into inch cube pieces – or slightly larger
2 inches of fresh root ginger in matchstick sized pieces
2 medium sized onions in lengthwise strips
6 long green chillies in lengthwise strips
2 tsp black peppercorns, crushed coarsely

4 tbsp malt vinegar
1/2 tsp of salt
8 tbsp vegetable oil

Place the onion, chilli, ginger, lamb together with the pepper and the vinegar in a bowl.
Knead it all together, squeezing by hand for 5 minutes.
Cover and leave in the fridge overnight.

Next day, put the contents of the bowl into a saucepan on full heat. Add no water. Cover with a tight lid. Cook for 10 to 12 minutes, stirring occasionally.
Drain the liquid, add salt and save for use later.
Put half of the contents of the saucepan into a frying pan with 4 tablespoons of oil and cook until the onions are brown.
Do the same with the other half.
Remove the meat from the frying pan and put all of it into the serving dish, then add to the frying pan the liquor you saved and bring to the boil.
Pour over the meat and serve.
Optional – garnish with a few oven potato chips.

Sambar

Serves 6
This is a very popular vegetarian dish from Tamil Nadu.
You may add a huge variety of vegetables to this dish.

For stage 1
200g red lentils
2 large red peppers
6 small round aubergines with ½" slit or 1 large aubergine in 2"
cubes.
2 large carrots in 1" sticks
3 tbsp powdered sambar masala
6 cloves garlic
1 ½ onions in large pieces
¼ tsp turmeric
2 green chillies slit in half

For stage 2
2 tbsp vegetable oil
1 ½ tsp tamarind
1 tsp mustard seeds
1/10th tsp asafoetida
8 curry leaves
1 tsp salt
1 onion, finely chopped

Stage1

Soak the lentils for ¼ hour, and rinse several times until the
water is much less cloudy.
Put the lentils in a large saucepan
Add half a pint of water and the turmeric, chillies and onions.
Cook on medium heat for 15 to 20 minutes then add another
200ml of water.
(Care: the mixture can froth. Keep an eye. If necessary, reduce
heat and remove the froth with a spoon. The frothing stops after
a few minutes)

Put the carrots into a small saucepan with 15 fl oz of water and bring to the boil, then add the aubergines and cook until they are translucent.
Add the aubergine and carrot, with the liquid, to the main pan with the lentils in.
Add the sambar masala, salt and tamarind juice.Mix and heat for 2 minutes on low heat, and then stand to one side.

Stage2

Heat the oil in a large frying pan and burst the mustard seeds.
Add onion and fry until brown.
Add the asafoetida and curry leaves.
Fry one more minute then add to the main pan.

Kollam Chicken Curry

Serves 6 to 8

Kollam , known during the days of British Raj as Quilon, is marked on the spice route.
Visit the Oriental Museum in Durham to see it!

1 Whole chicken (about 1.5 kg) skinned and chopped into pieces
2 medium onions, coarsely chopped
3 chillies, roughly chopped
1 tsp chilli powder
3 tbsp coriander powder
6 cinnamon sticks
12 cloves.
1 ½ tbsp garam masala
1 tsp turmeric powder
1 heaped tbsp white poppy seeds
1 ½ inches root ginger.
10 cloves garlic
4 tbsp vegetable oil
400g can of chopped tomato
1 tsp salt
2tbsp oil

Soak the poppy seeds in water for ten minutes.
Peel and chop the garlic and ginger and grind to a paste.
(Poppy seeds, chilli, garlic and ginger can be ground in a blender)
Put oil in a large saucepan on medium heat, add the cinnamon, cloves and onion when oil is warm.
Cook until onion is translucent.

Add the poppy seeds, chilli, garlic and ginger mixture and cook on a low heat for 5 minutes stirring occasionally.

Add the coriander powder, garam masala, chilli powder and turmeric.

Stir well and add the tomato.

Gently increase to medium heat, add the chicken and make sure it is mixed well or it will stick.

Add 150ml of water.

Cover with a tight lid and cook on low heat for 25 minutes (you will notice that by this time the oil will separate out).

Add the salt.

Remove from heat and leave to stand for half an hour.

Leela's Beef Curry
Serves 6

People who are Hindus do not eat beef as the cow is a sacred animal, according to their belief. Tamil Nadu population is predominantly Hindu and beef is not readily available in small towns. Kerala has a large Christian population and beef is consumed in great quantity. Occasionally, beef was brought to Beena's mother's house by visitors . They never let their Tamil friends know this as they did not want to hurt their feelings. This is a recipe Beena's sister Leela remembered.

1 kg braising steak
½ inch of cinnamon stick
6 cloves
2 heaped dessert spoons chilli powder
2 fl oz malt vinegar
3 medium onions in ½" squares
2 tbsp coriander powder
2 tbsp cumin powder
1 tsp salt
3 tbsp vegetable oil

Cut beef into 2 inch squares and put in a large bowl. Crush cloves and cinnamon and add to the beef.
Add chilli powder and vinegar. Knead well and leave to marinade overnight.
Next day, put in saucepan with 2 tablespoons of water and cook with the lid on, at a low heat for one hour.
Strain the beef and save the liquid.
Heat the oil in a saucepan to a high heat and add onions and cook until translucent. –for about 10 minutes.
Add the coriander and the cumin. Mix it well or it will stick – cook for about 3 minutes then add a teaspoon of chilli powder.
Add the beef and mix well. Add the salt and the beef liquid, replace lid and cook on medium heat for 5 to 10 minutes.

Kerala Fish Curry

Serves 6

6 pieces of salmon/cod etc
5 cloves garlic, finely chopped
1 onion, sliced lengthwise
4 green chillies cut lengthwise
1 inch ginger in matchstick size pieces
6 large tomatoes in 1/8th pieces
1/3rd tsp turmeric
½ tsp salt
3 tbsp oil

In a large pan, fry the onion in oil on a high heat, until it is translucent.
Add ginger and garlic.
Reduce heat to half.
Cook for 2 minutes then add the chilli.
Cook until onion starts to turn brown, then add tomatoes.
Cover and reduce heat further.
Cook for 15 minutes then add 2 tablespoons of water and the turmeric.
Add salt and stir the mixture.
Add the slices of fish.
Cover with the sauce and then cover with the lid and cook for 15 minutes.

Aromatic Egg Curry

Serves 6

7 eggs
2 small onions, coarsely chopped
¼ tsp chilli powder
3x 1" cinnamon sticks
1 tbsp garam masala
5 cloves
1 dsp curry powder
1 black cardamom pod
¼ tsp turmeric
5 bay leaves
1 tsp fennel, dry roasted and crushed to a powder
2 x 400 g tins chopped tomatoes
150 g potatoes, in 1" cubes
1½ tsp salt

Hard boil the eggs and cool quickly in cold water.
Heat pan and add 2 tablespoons of oil.
Add onion, cinnamon, cloves and cardamom.
Cook on medium to low heat until the onion is translucent.

Add potato, then the bay leaves.
Fry for 5 minutes stirring occasionally.
Add chilli powder, turmeric, garam masala and curry powder.
Fry for 5 more minutes.
Add tomato, the powdered fennel and salt. Mix, cover and cook for 15 minutes.
Shell and halve the eggs, place in the sauce yolk up, spooning some sauce over the top.
Heat gently, for at least 5 minutes.

Red Lentil Dhal

Serves 6

200g red split lentils
1 medium onion finely chopped
4 tomatoes in 1" cubes
1 tbsp oil
1 ½ tsp mustard seeds
1 tbsp coriander powder
½ tsp chilli powder
Salt

Soak lentils for half an hour and rinse until water becomes less cloudy.
Cook in one pint of water for half an hour or until they become a mush.
Heat oil in pan and burst the mustard seeds. Add the onion & fry until caramelised.
Add coriander powder and chilli powder. Stir them to mix.
Add the tomatoes and cook on medium heat until tomatoes soften.
Add the lentil and its liquid and salt to taste.
Garnish with coriander leaves before serving.

Mince Kheema

Serves 6

500g beef mince
8 cloves garlic and 1" root ginger crushed to a paste
1 tsp ground nutmeg
½ tbsp garam masala
½ tbsp cumin powder
1 tbsp coriander powder
1 tsp chilli powder
1 tsp cinnamon powder
1 tsp mixed spice
15 cashew nuts
1 medium onion, finely chopped
200g peas
1 ½ tbsp tomato puree
1 tbsp oil

Heat oil in a pan and fry the onion and garlic-ginger paste until
the onion is translucent.
Add the garam masala, cumin and coriander powders and fry for
one more minute.

Then add the powders of chilli, mixed spice, cinnamon and nutmeg and stir well and cook for between 30 seconds and a minute.
Add the mince and tomato puree.
Reduce heat to medium and stir thoroughly to combine.
Add 2 tbsp boiling water and cook with lid on, above a low heat for 10 minutes.
Chop cashew nuts into quarters and add to the pan with the peas and tomato puree.
Cook for another 10 minutes.
The total cooking time is about 25 minutes.

Chicken pepper fry

Serves 6

1.5 kg whole chicken chopped into large pieces
2 tsp powdered black pepper
1 tsp cumin powder
2 tbsp soy sauce
½ tsp garam masala
6 medium onions, halved then finely sliced
1 tbsp ginger and garlic paste
1 tbsp vinegar
8 curry leaves (optional)
3 tbsp oil
2 green chillies, halved
1 tsp salt

Heat oil in pan, add onions and cook until light brown.
Add the garlic-ginger paste stirring continuously for 5 minutes.
Add the curry leaves (if using) and cook for 2 minutes.
Add the salt, garam masala, cumin and the pepper and cook for another 2 minutes.
Add the chicken and stir well.
Add 3 tbsp water.
Add the chillies with the vinegar.
Cover and cook on medium heat for 45 minutes by which time the water will be used up.
Add soy sauce and cook for another 10 minutes.
The total cooking time is about 55 minutes.

Ammachy's Cutlet

Serves 6

Beena called her mother Ammachy. It is the Malayalam word for mother.

450g potatoes, boiled and mashed
500g beef mince
1 ½ tsp fennel powder
1 ¼ tsp black pepper powder
1 ½ inches root ginger, grated
2 medium onions finely chopped
4 tbsp chopped coriander leaves
1 large green chilli finely chopped
1 ½ tsp salt
1 egg
Breadcrumb
1 tbsp oil

Put the mince in a pan with 2 tablespoons of water. Cook for 15 minutes on a medium heat, stirring occasionally. Drain liquid from the mince and stand to one side.

Heat oil in a pan and fry the onions until translucent then add the chilli, ginger and fennel.
Mix the mince, potato, pepper and coriander in a 2 litre bowl, then add the onion, chilli, ginger and fennel mixture from the frying pan. Mix all together by hand and allow to cool.
Form the mixture into balls (about twice the size of a golf ball) then form oval shapes.
Beat the egg and dip the ovals into it then coat with breadcrumb.
Wipe a non-stick pan with oil and fry both sides of the cutlets on a low heat/ or shallow fry in oil in an ordinary frying pan.

Chicken Biryani

Serves 8

Cooking oil
One medium sized chicken cut into 2 to 3 inch pieces (700g)
3 heaped tbsp chopped coriander leaves
2 heaped tbsp chopped mint
12 tbsp natural yoghurt
1 ½ tbsp ginger-garlic paste
3 dessert spoons "Biryani mix" (available from Asian food stores)
2 small red chillies
3 medium onions, halved and thinly sliced1
2 cashew nuts, quartered
30 raisins
600g rice (or 80% of the weight of the chicken)
8 cardamom pods, split
4 cinnamon sticks in 1" pieces (size is not critical)
2 tbsp pure butter ghee

Place the chicken, ginger-garlic, coriander, mint, 12 tbsp of the yoghurt and the biryani mix into a 2 litre bowl.
Mix up and let it marinade for at least half an hour.
Fill a saucepan with oil to half inch depth and heat.
Cook the onion in the oil until brown (you may need to do this in two batches). Reserve a little of this to use as a garnish.
This will take about 20 minutes per batch.
Decant into a colander lined with kitchen paper.

Boil the rice for 4 minutes and then drain.

Into a large saucepan put 2 tbsp oil and 2 tbsp of ghee and heat.
Break cardamom pods and add to the oil, followed by the cinnamon sticks and fry for one minute.
Add the chillies and the chicken mixture to the hot oil and mix around.
Cover and cook for 5 minutes.

Take a large pan with a tight fitting lid.
Grease the pan with oil.
Place half of the chicken mix at the bottom.
Top it with half of the crispy onion and follow it by one half of the rice.
Continue to layer using the second half of each mixture.
Cover tightly and cook on medium to low heat for 10 minutes.
Reduce heat to low and cook for a further 35 minutes.
Remove from heat and stir it all up.

The garnish
Fry the cashew nuts and raisins in oil or butter. Cook for 2 minutes, mix with the reserved crispy onions and use as a garnish.

Potato and Pea Bhaji

Serves 6

2 large potatoes boiled, skinned and diced in ½" cubes
½ medium onion, finely chopped
1 small green chilli, coarsely chopped
1 inch root ginger, finely chopped or grated
200g frozen peas
1 tbsp oil
1 tsp mustard seeds
¼ tsp turmeric
Juice of lime or lemon
½ tsp salt

Heat the oil in a pan and burst the mustard seeds, then add the onion and ginger.
Fry, until translucent.
Add turmeric then the chilli. Cook for 2 minutes until onions have browned.
Then add the peas.
Reduce heat to medium, cover and cook for 5 minutes.
Mix in the potato and salt.
Add 4 tablespoons of water and leave on low heat for 2 minutes, then mix in 4 teaspoons of lime or lemon juice, and serve.

Malayalee Fish Curry

Serves 4

2 trout or sea bream
2 ½ tsp turmeric powder
1 ½ tsp chilli powder
1 ½ tsp salt
Oil
1 medium onion coarsely chopped
1 inch root ginger grated
4 cloves garlic sliced thinly
1 globe fennel sliced in thick pieces
100g coconut cream
2 medium size red chillies slit lengthwise
1/10th tsp fenugreek powder
1 dessert spoon tomato puree
1 tsp lemon juice
8 curry leaves

Remove gills and fins from the fish and cut into three inch sections.
Slice at one inch intervals, both sides, almost to the bone.

Mix the turmeric, chilli powder and salt with 20 ml of water and make a stiff paste.
Rub the paste into the slits and inside of the fish.

Heat oil in a frying pan, on high heat – sufficient to shallow fry – and add the fish.
Set heat to medium and cook for 5 minutes turning once
Remove the fish from the pan to a tray lined with kitchen towel to absorb excess oil..
Drain the oil from the pan leaving only 3 tbsp behind.

Heat the oil and fry the onion for 2 minutes then add the chillies, ginger, garlic, fenugreek powder, ½ tsp turmeric and the fennel. Cook on medium heat for 5 minutes then add the tomato puree and 200 ml of water.
Cook with lid on for 12 minutes.
Add coconut cream, 1 tsp salt, the lemon juice and the curry leaves.

Add the fish and cook on low heat with lid on for 20 minutes, turning once.

Sornam's Lamb with Aubergine

Serves 6.

In Tamil Nadu, non-vegetarians celebrated weddings with the meat from a goat. This dish was prepared for breakfast for the morning after the wedding. The left over meat-with-bones was used in this dish. The pot was allowed to cook in the dying embers overnight.   Sornam was the family cook

1 kg lamb chops
2 medium onions finely chopped
50g lamb seasoning
12 small aubergines with a 1cm slit at the end
3 ½ tbsp garam masala
3 ½ tbsp oil
2 medium sized green chillies with ends slit(about ½")
¼ tsp chilli powder

Sprinkle the lamb seasoning over the lamb and leave for at least one hour.
Heat the oil in a pan to a high heat and cook the onions until translucent.

Reduce heat to medium and add the aubergines – cover and cook for 15 minutes stirring occasionally.
Add the garam masala and cook for another 3 minutes.
Then add the lamb and mix well.
Stir in 250ml of boiling water, cover and cook on a **low heat** for 15 minutes.
Add to the pot.
Cover and cook for a further 1 ½ hours.
Skim off as much of the surface oil as possible before serving.

Meat Ball Curry (Kofta)

Serves 6

1 kg beef mince
1 ½ tbsp garam masala
1 ½ medium onions, finely chopped
2 x 400g tins chopped tomatoes
2 inches cinnamon stick
2 star aniseed
2 tbsp curry powder
5 bay leaves
5 cloves
2 tbsp oil
2 tbsp ginger-garlic paste
1 tsp salt

Add garam masala to the mince in a 2 litre bowl and knead well.
Form the mixture into golf ball sized spheres.
Heat oil in a pan and fry the onions until translucent, then add
the cinnamon, cloves, star aniseed, ginger-garlic paste and bay
leaves.
Reduce heat to medium and cook until the mixture begins to
brown – about 10 minutes.

Add curry powder and then the chopped tomatoes. Mix well.
Cover and increase heat to bring to the boil.
Reduce heat and simmer gently for 5 minutes. Add salt and
100ml of boiling water.

Place the meat balls in the mixture, cover and cook on a low
heat for 30 minutes.
Garnish with coriander leaves and serve.

Hilda's Bangalore Venison

Serves 8

1 kg venison, cubed
2 large onions, chopped
5 large tomatoes, chopped
2 tbsp tomato puree
2 tbsp coriander powder
2 tbsp curry powder
1 tsp turmeric
2 tsp mustard seeds
juice of half a lemon
1 cup of coconut milk
25g fresh coriander
250g okra, in thirds
250g shallots, halved
1 ½ tsp salt
2 tbsp oil
1 tbsp ginger-garlic paste

Marinade the venison in the lemon juice and tomato puree for a few hours.

Preheat oven to 180°C.

Heat oil in a large pan and burst the mustard seeds.
Cook onion until caramelised then add the ginger-garlic paste
and keep stirring while adding turmeric, curry powder and
coriander powder.
Fry for 3 minutes.

Add the venison and its marinade, and the salt.
Transfer to an oven proof dish, cover and cook in the oven for 45
minutes.

Remove, from the oven, add the coconut milk and mix.
Top with the shallots, tomatoes and okra; press down, cover and
continue cooking in the oven for another 25 minutes.

Remove from the oven, mix in the coriander leaves and cook for
a further 5 minutes.

Curried chicken with potato

Serves 8

1 medium sized chicken chopped into large pieces
500g potatoes, in quarters
2 medium onions, finely chopped
5 tbsp coriander powder
3 tbsp cumin powder
¼ tsp turmeric
1 tsp chilli powder
1 tsp powdered cloves
½ tsp cinnamon powder
½ tsp mixed spice
2 tbsp garam masala
4 tbsp oil
3 tbsp ginger-garlic paste
3 tbsp yoghurt
2 tsp salt

Put the oil into a large saucepan and fry the onions slowly until translucent.
Add the powders of the coriander, cumin, turmeric, chilli, cloves, cinnamon, mixed spice and garam masala.
Fry for 5 minutes over a low heat.

Add 100ml of water and stir.

Add ginger-garlic paste then add the chicken and stir well to ensure it is coated with the mixture.

Cover and cook for 5 minutes.

Now add the potatoes and cook for another 5 minutes stirring occasionally.

Add another 100 ml of water, cover and cook for 40 minutes on a low heat.

Finally, mix in the yoghurt and salt and cook over a medium heat until the oil separates – this should be about another 15 minutes.

Curried Kippers

Serves 4

4 kippers, or any other smoked fish, heads and tails   removed
2 medium onions
2 x 400g tins of plum tomatoes, chopped.
3 tbsp garlic-ginger paste
1 tbsp fennel seeds, crushed
3 medium sized green chillies, finely chopped
1 tsp salt
1 tsp paprika
2 tbsp oil

Heat the oil in a pan and fry the onion until translucent.
Add the fennel, chillies and garlic-ginger paste and fry for 5 minutes.
 Add the tomato and the salt, and bring to the boil.
Cook for 2 minutes and then add the fish and paprika.
Cook on a medium heat for 5 minutes.

SIDE DISHES

Aubergine with Tamarind

Serves 6

2 large aubergines in ½" cubes
2 tsp tamarind pulp
1/5th tsp asafoetida
2 tsp chilli powder
1 tsp turmeric
2 tsp fenugreek seeds
1 dsp tomato puree
2 tsp cumin seeds
2 tsp cumin powder
8 tbsp oil
4 fresh tomatoes in 1/8th pieces
½ tsp brown sugar
1 tsp salt

Heat a deep frying pan and add the oil.
Add cumin seeds and cook on high heat until brown.

Add aubergine pieces. Stir well for 3 minutes.
Reduce heat to medium for one minute, then to low for one minute.

Add the fenugreek seeds, turmeric, cumin powder and chilli powder.

Increase heat to medium and stir for 2 minutes then add the asafoetida and the tomato puree.
Add the chopped tomato and salt, then mix well and reduce heat to low. Cover and cook for 5 minutes.

Take one level teaspoon of the tamarind pulp and mix with a tablespoon of water. Add to the pan.
Stir in the brown sugar.

Let it stand for ten minutes then serve.

Yoghurt Curry

Serves 8

1 ½ onions, finely chopped
1 tsp mustard seeds
Oil
500g fat free yoghurt
3 fl oz water
½ tsp turmeric powder
½ tsp salt
¼ tsp chilli powder
4 to 6 small red chillies according to taste
8 curry leaves

Mix the water and yoghurt in a bowl with the turmeric and chilli powders and salt.

Heat frying pan and add a dessert spoon of oil.
When hot, burst the mustard seeds, add onions and fry with stirring, on high heat until caramelised.
Add the chillies and the curry leaves.

Turn heat off and stand for 2 minutes.
Then add the yoghurt and mix well.

Strain out the solid bits and serve cold over rice.

Sag Aloo

Serves 6

500g spinach
5 medium sized boiled potatoes in ½ "cubes
1 medium onion finely chopped
1 heaped tsp cumin seeds
2 tbsp vegetable oil
6 garlic cloves, finely chopped
2 heaped tsp curry powder
5 red chillies, small
1 tsp salt

Cook the spinach in the microwave.
Heat oil in a deep frying pan and add cumin seeds. Fry for a
minute until brown then add the onion.
Stir for a minute until the onion starts to brown then add the
garlic. Stir above a high heat until golden brown.
Add curry powder and chillies and stir for another 2 minutes.
Add the potatoes and salt, mix and fry for 2 minutes. Take off
the heat and add the spinach, mix and cook for about a minute.
Serve.

Optional - as a final addition at the same time as adding the
spinach, put in one tablespoon of coconut milk.

Thoran Cabbage

Serves 6

1 medium cabbage   any variety, finely shredded
2 heaped tbsp desiccated coconut
½ tsp turmeric
4 cloves garlic
1 tsp cumin seeds
1 medium sized onion, finely chopped
¾ tbsp oil
½ tsp mustard seeds
1 tsp salt
2 green chillies
½ teaspoon salt

Place the cabbage in a 2 litre bowl.
Crush the garlic, cumin seeds and chillies in a mortar with a pestle.
Mix the coconut with turmeric and 2 tablespoons of boiling water.
Add **all** to the cabbage and mix.
Put in a saucepan with 1 tablespoon of water and the salt.
Cook on medium heat for 2 to 3 minutes.

Heat oil in a frying pan, burst the mustard seeds and then add the onion and cook until caramelised.

Add the cabbage, mix well and cook for 2 minutes.

Mizhukku Peratti (Brahmin's Beans)

Serves 6

500g fine green beans in 1" pieces
2 tsp salt
1 onion in ¼" cubes
6 to 9 small dry red chillies according to taste
1 tsp mustard seeds
¾ tbsp oil

Boil the beans with the salt for 5 minutes then drain.

Place the onion and the chillies in a mortar and crush.

Heat oil in a deep frying pan and burst mustard seeds.
Add the crushed mixture and fry for 5 minutes until onion
caramelises.
Add beans and mix, and fry for 2 to 3 minutes.

Tofu and Red Pepper

Serves 6

250g tofu drained (either smoked or un-smoked) in 1" squares
2 large red peppers cut in narrow strips
2 large green chillies, halved lengthwise
¼ tsp chilli powder
1 ½ tsp garam masala
6 cloves garlic, in slices
1 tsp dark soy sauce
1 large onion cut lengthwise
4 fresh tomatoes, deseeded and cut in 1/8ths
2 tbsp oil
50g leaf spinach

Place the tofu in a bowl and sprinkle the garam masala over it.
Leave it aside for an hour, if there is time.

Heat oil in a deep frying pan, add onion and cook until
translucent. Add the garlic and cook for a further 2 minutes.

Add the tofu and peppers, stir and cover.
Cook for 5 minutes.

Add chillies and cook for 3 minutes.
Add tomatoes and stir gently ensuring that the tofu pieces
do not break-up.
Add the chilli powder, reduce heat and cover.
Cook until soft – about quarter of an hour (or a shorter time
for a crunchy texture).

Add the soy sauce and a handful of spinach and mix.
Cook for only one more minute before serving.

Peppered Cauliflower

Serves 6
½ tbsp peppercorns crushed coarsely
1 tbsp oil
¼ tsp salt
1 tsp cumin seeds
½ onion finely chopped
1 medium sized cauliflower in small florets

Heat the oil in a pan.
Add onion and cook until translucent, then add cumin seeds.
Add cauliflower and stir then add pepper, salt and one
tablespoon of water.

Put the lid on and cook on a low heat for about 20 minutes.

Loufer.

Serves 6

This is an unusual vegetable found only in Asian food stores

3 loufers
165ml coconut milk
½ onion, coarsely chopped
2 chillies, sliced lengthwise
2 cardamom pods, crushed slightly
1 ½ tsp mustard seeds
10 black peppercorns
3 cloves
1" long cinnamon stick
½ tsp turmeric
1 tsp fennel seeds

Peel the loufer, slice and chop.
Heat oil in a deep frying pan and burst the mustard seeds in it.
Add the onion and fry until the onion starts to brown.
Stir in the turmeric.
Mix together broken cardamom pods, black peppercorns, cloves and the cinnamon and fennel seeds and add to the frying pan. Cook for a minute.
Add green chillies salt and the loufer.
Add one tablespoon of water and cook on a very low heat for about 25 minutes.
Finally, stir in the coconut milk.

Courgette Salad

Serves 6

1 large courgette, grated
1 inch root ginger, grated finely
1 tsp vegetable oil
1 tsp cumin seeds
1/2 tsp salt
1 tbsp desiccated coconut
250g yoghurt
Paprika

Squeeze the water out of the courgette.
Heat oil in a frying pan, add cumin seeds and fry until brown.
Add the ginger and coconut and fry until the coconut is brown.
Add the courgette and turn the heat off.
Mix up but do not cook any more.
Mix in the salt and yoghurt.
Sprinkle paprika as a garnish.

Uppuma
Serves 8

150g coarse semolina
1 inch root ginger finely chopped
2 long green chillies, finely chopped
12 curry leaves
1 tbsp vegetable oil
16g butter
1 tsp mustard seeds
½ tsp salt

Heat a deep frying pan and add semolina (note, no oil at this stage).
Roast for 2 minutes.

Heat oil in another frying pan and burst the mustard seeds in it. Then add the ginger, chilli and curry leaves, and fry for about a minute.

To this, add 450ml of boiling water.
Now, add the semolina and stir vigorously.
Cover and leave for 5 minutes, then stir in the butter.

Kalai's Beetroot
Serves 6

4 raw beetroot (medium sized), grated
½ onion, finely chopped
1½ tsp curry powder
3 tbsp desiccated coconut
1 tbsp oil
¼ tsp salt
1/8 tsp chilli powder

Heat the oil in a deep pan.
Cook the onion until brown.
Add curry powder, chilli powder, coconut, and the beetroot.
Cook for 5 minutes then add salt. Cover and cook for another 5 minutes. Leave for 5 minutes before serving.

Tuet *Green Banana*

Serves 6

This is an unusual vegetable found only in Asian food stores

4 raw green bananas
½ onion coarsely chopped
4 dried chillies
½ tsp salt

*(Caution: Oil the hands prior to handling the green banana.
This will help prevent stickiness and staining.
The sap is not harmful!)*

Peel and cut the bananas in quarters, then to one inch lengths
and put in cold water straight away to avoid blackening.
Crush the chopped onion and chillies.
Put the bananas into a pan of water and boil until soft (8 to 10
minutes) then drain.
Heat 1 tbsp of oil in a pan and fry the onion-chilli mix until the
onion is caramelised.
Add the banana and salt, mix and fry for 2 minutes.
Keep stirring with care to prevent excessive breaking up of the
banana pieces.

Spiced Butternut Squash

Serves 6

1 x 600g butternut squash
1 tsp mustard seeds
1 medium onion, coarsely chopped
1 large green chilli, finely chopped
2 tsp curry powder
3 tbsp desiccated coconut
1 tbsp vegetable oil
1 tsp salt

Cut the squash into quarters and remove the seeds.
Cut off the rind and chop the squash into ½ inch cubes.
Rinse and microwave on full power for 6 to 8 minutes.
Add a little boiling water to the coconut and set aside.
Burst the mustard seeds in a pan of hot oil.
Add the onion and cook until caramelised.
Add the curry powder, chilli and coconut.
Fry for 1 minute.
Add the butternut squash and salt.
Cover, and cook on low heat for 20 minutes, turning frequently.

Roasted Aubergine Salad
Serves 6

2 medium sized aubergines
350 to 400g thick plain yogurt
1green chilli, deseeded and coarsely chopped
½" fresh ginger, grated
4 spring onions in ¼ inch pieces
A small bunch of fresh coriander leaves, finely chopped
1tsp chunky chat masala

Pre-heat the oven to 200°C.

Cut the aubergines into half lengthwise and slice into ½ inch
cubes taking care not to cut through the outer skin.
Drizzle with olive oil and rub it in.
Cover with foil and place on a baking tray in the oven for 30
minutes.

Remove from the oven and leave to cool.

In a 2 litre bowl, mix the yoghurt, chilli, ginger and spring onions.
Remove the flesh from the baked aubergines and add to the mix.
Mix in the chunky chat masala.

Spinach with Paneer
Serves 6

500g spinach
½ inch root ginger
5 cloves garlic
100g paneer in ½" cubes
2 tbsp oil
1 tbsp coriander powder
1 tsp cumin seeds
1 medium onion finely chopped.
1 medium sized chilli coarsely chopped
¼ tsp chilli powder
½ tsp salt

Cook and when cool, puree the spinach in a blender.

Heat 1tablespoonful oil in pan and fry the paneer until browned, then transfer to a bowl for later use.

Crush together the onion, garlic and ginger in a mortar.

In a separate pan, fry the cumin seeds in the remaining oil for one minute, then add the crushed paste and the chilli.
On a low heat, fry for 5 minutes and add the coriander and chilli powders.
Cook for 2 more minutes.
Stir periodically to prevent sticking.

Add the paneer and mix together.
Finally, mix in the spinach and salt.

Cover and cook for 5 minutes on a low heat.

Mixed Vegetable-Aviyal

Serves 6

2 green bananas
3 murunga (commonly known as "drumsticks")
1 carrot
2 small potatoes
3 chembu
5 small aubergines
¼ gourd
2 green chillies
1 medium onion sliced lengthwise
6 tbsp desiccated coconut
½ tsp turmeric
5 cloves garlic
1 ½ tsp cumin powder
2 green mangoes (seasonal until June)
20 curry leaves
1 ½ tsp salt

Soak the coconut in 2 tablespoonfuls of warm water for an hour and then mix in the turmeric.

Crush the garlic, cumin and chilli to make a course mixture.

Peel and chop all the vegetables to one inch cubes (put the aubergines and green banana in water to prevent discolouration).

Boil the chembu for 10 minutes and discard the water and then rinse with some cold water.

Boil the murunga for 5 minutes in 250ml water in a saucepan.

Add all the vegetables except the gourd to the murunga in the saucepan and bring back to the boil.

After 10 minutes put the gourd in.

Grind the coconut in a blender and mix it with the garlic/chilli/cumin. Transfer this mixture and the chembu to the pan of vegetables. Add curry leaves.

Continue to boil for another 10 minutes.

Finally, mix in one tablespoon of oil and leave to stand for 5 minutes then serve.

Chilli Ka Salam

Serves 6

1 ½ tbsp smooth peanut butter
2 tbsp Tahini
7 large light green chillies (or large yellow peppers if unavailable)
1 large green pepper sliced to 1 inch squares.
1 ½ tsp tamarind pulp
1 tbsp coriander powder
½ tsp cumin powder
1 ½ tbsp coriander leaves, chopped
¼ tsp turmeric
1 onion, coarsely chopped
1 ½ tsp ginger-garlic paste

3 tbsp oil
½ tsp sugar
Note: The chillies used here should be a non pungent variety

Mix peanut butter, tahini and tamarind with ¼ cup of water.
Cut chillies to 1 inch rounds and remove seeds.
Heat oil in a pan and add chillies, pepper, onion and cook for 10 minutes on medium heat.
Add the garlic-ginger paste, the peanut butter-turmeric-tamarind mixture, coriander powder, cumin powder and 2 cups of water.
Cook on low heat for 10 minutes.
Finally, add 1 tsp salt, coriander leaves and sugar.
Total cooking time is about 30 minutes.

Okra

Serves 6

300 g Okra (ladies fingers) in ¾" lengths
1 ½ onions halved then finely sliced
1 tsp crushed black peppercorns
2 tbsp oil
1 ½ tsp cumin seeds
1 dsp curry powder
1/10th tsp asafoetida

Heat oil in a frying pan and add onions, cumin seeds, pepper and curry powder.
Fry for 5 minutes.

Sprinkle the asafoetida and add the okra.
Mix and cook on low heat for 20 minutes.

Dhal Curry

Serves 6

200g toor dhal (red lentil can be substituted)
¼ tsp turmeric
1 tbsp ginger-garlic paste
1 medium onion, finely chopped
2 tsp curry powder
1 tsp salt,
1 tsp cumin seeds
4 tomatoes finely chopped
50g creamed coconut
1 tbsp oil

Soak the toor dhal for half an hour then rinse thoroughly and drain.
Cook in one pint of water for 10 minutes.
Add turmeric and the salt. Reduce heat, cover and cook for 1¼ hours.

Mix the coconut with a little hot water and add it to the dhal.

Heat the oil in a pan and brown the cumin seeds.
Add the onion and the ginger-garlic paste and cook until brown.
Add the curry powder, tomatoes and coconut and cook for 30 minutes.
Add this to the dhal.
Mix thoroughly.

Garnish with coriander leaves and serve.

Vegetable Stew

Serves 6

125g runner beans in 2" lengths
250g carrots quartered, then in 1" pieces
200g potatoes in 1" pieces
1 medium onion, coarsely chopped
1 inch ginger in matchstick size pieces
6 cloves
1 tsp black peppercorns
6 bay leaves
5 baby leeks
1 tbsp oil
3 x one inch cinnamon sticks
½ pint boiling water
1 ½ tsp salt
4 cardamom pods
1 large red chilli slit half-way lengthwise
¼ tsp turmeric
4 tomatoes

Cut leeks to 2 inch lengths, then in half lengthwise
Heat the oil to medium heat then add to it onion, leeks, ginger, cinnamon, peppercorns, chilli, cardamom, cloves, bay leaves, carrots, potatoes and salt. Add the boiling water, and let the mixture come to the boil.
Then reduce heat to low, cover and cook for 15 minutes until the potatoes and carrots soften.
Now add the beans. Cover and cook for 5 more minutes.

There will be leek leaves left over.
These can be fried in oil and added to any accompanying rice dish.

Spicy Ladies Fingers

Serves 4

200g Okra
½ tsp turmeric
½ tsp chilli powder
1 tsp cumin powder
1 tsp garam masala
½ tsp salt
3 large tomatoes, halved, deseeded and in ½" squares
½ a medium onion finely chopped
3 tbsp oil
1 tsp onion seeds

Wipe the okra with kitchen roll and slit to within half an inch of the ends.
Fill the slits with a mixture made from the turmeric, chilli powder, cumin powder.
Set to one side for half an hour.

Heat the oil and add the onion and onion seeds.
Fry on a high heat until translucent.

Add tomatoes and garam masala.
Reduce heat to medium.
Add ½ tsp salt and continue the cooking with occasional stirring

After 5 minutes, add the okra and stir.
Cover, reduce heat to low and cook for 20 minutes.

Serve with a garnish of coriander leaves.

.

Spinach in Coconut Milk

Serves 6

600g spinach
6 cloves garlic finely chopped
1 medium onion finely chopped
3 small red chillies
165 ml coconut milk
2 tbsp oil
1 tsp mustard seeds
1 tsp curry powder
½ tsp salt

Heat oil in a pan and burst the mustard seeds.
Add onion and cook until translucent, then add the garlic, curry powder, and chillies.
Cook for 2 minutes on low heat then add the spinach. Increase heat, cover and cook for 10 minutes.
Add salt and the coconut milk.
Reduce heat, cover and cook for another 10 minutes.

Cly's Curly Kale

Serves 6

250g curly kale
1 tsp mustard seeds
2 tbsp desiccated coconut
1 tsp cumin seeds
1 tsp pepper corns
1½ tbsp oil
½ tsp turmeric
½ tsp salt
75g frozen cooked prawns

Blanch the kale in boiling water for 2 minutes then chop finely.
Coarsely crush peppercorns and cumin seeds using a mortar
and pestle.
Heat oil in a pan and burst the mustard seeds.
Add kale and the coconut, the turmeric and the crushed cumin-
pepper mixture. Stir.
Cook on a high heat for 2 minutes. Reduce heat, add the salt
and 1 tablespoon of water, cover and cook for 10 minutes.
Add the prawns, mix and allow to stand on the hot cooker for 2
minutes with a lid on. Then serve.

Dadhima's Aloo Gobi

Serves 6

1 large or 2 medium bay leaves
1 inch of grated root ginger
1 medium cauliflower in 1" cubes
1 tbsp coriander powder
½ tsp chilli powder
½ tsp turmeric
1/10th tsp asafoetida
2 tbsp oil
1 medium sized fresh red/green chilli, slit
350g unpeeled potatoes
1½ tsp chunky chat masala
1 tsp salt

Scrub, wash and cut the unpeeled potato into half inch slices.
Mix to a paste the coriander powder, chilli powder, turmeric and grated ginger with 1 tbsp water.
Heat the oil in a pan, add asafoetida and bay leaves and cook for one minute, then add the paste.
Add the chilli together with the potato, cauliflower and 100 ml of water. Cook on medium heat for 5 minutes.
Add the salt and another 50 ml of water.
Cover and cook for 20 minutes.
Sprinkle in the chunky chat masala, mix well and stand for five minutes before serving.

Okra in coconut milk

Serves 4

25 to 30 okra
1 onion, finely chopped
1½ tbsp oil
1 tsp mustard seeds
1 tbsp ginger-garlic paste
2 medium sized green chillies slit half way lengthwise
½ tsp turmeric
20 black peppercorns coarsely crushed
50g pure creamed coconut

Top and tail the okra and cut to one inch lengths.
Heat the oil in a pan and burst the mustard seeds.
Add the onion and ginger-garlic paste and cook until the onion is translucent.
Add the okra, the chilli and turmeric and cook on a low heat for 15 minutes, then increase heat to medium, add the pepper, cover and cook for a further 15 minutes.
Add boiling water to the creamed coconut to make to 8 fl oz, pour over the okra, mix well, cook for a further 30 seconds and serve.

Payaru with French Beans

Serves 6

100g mung beans
500g French beans in ½" lengths
4 cloves garlic
1 tsp cumin seeds
2 tbsp desiccated coconut
1 medium sized red chilli
½ tsp turmeric
1 tsp salt
½ medium size onion
1 tbsp oil
1 tsp mustard seeds
10 curry leaves

Soak coconut in 2 tbsp boiling water.
Boil mung beans for half an hour until soft.
Crush the garlic, cumin seeds and chilli with a mortar and pestle.
Boil the French beans until almost soft.
Drain the French beans and add the crushed mixture, the coconut, turmeric and salt. Mix well.
Cover and cook on medium heat for 15 minutes stirring frequently.
Add the mung beans, mix and turn off the heat.
Heat oil in a pan and burst the mustard seeds.
Add onion and cook until caramelised.
Add curry leaves and then the beans mixture.
Ensure that the ingredients are mixed well. Serve.

Radish "47"

Serves 6

300g radishes, grated
200g carrots, grated
4 tsp lime juice
½ tsp cumin seeds
½ tsp mustard seeds
½ onion finely chopped
½ tsp salt
1 large green chilli, coarsely chopped

Heat oil in a pan and burst the mustard seeds.
Add cumin seeds and heat until the cumin starts to brown.
Turn heat off and add the radish, carrot and the onion.
Mix well.
Finally, mix in the lime juice, salt and chilli.
Serve.

Cabbage and chick pea flour
Serves 4

300g shredded cabbage
1 tbsp gram flour
2 tbsp oil
½ tsp cumin seeds
½ tsp mustard seeds
½ tsp chilli powder
½ tsp turmeric
¼ tsp fenugreek seeds
1 tsp fennel seeds
½ tsp salt

Heat oil in a pan and burst the mustard seeds.
Add cumin seeds, fenugreek, fennel, chilli powder, turmeric and
fry on low heat for about 2 minutes. Then add the cabbage.
Add the gram flour by passing through a fine sieve.
Stir to ensure a good mixing.
Add salt, cover and cook on a low heat for 15 minutes, then add
a dessert spoonful of water.
Mix, cook for another 2 minutes, then serve.

Peas with Paneer, South Indian Style

Serves 6

150g paneer, grated
500g peas
1 medium onion finely chopped
1 tsp garam masala
1 heaped tsp curry powder
1 tbsp oil
1 tsp mustard seeds
½ tsp salt
3 medium tomatoes, chopped
2 tbsp chopped coriander
1 tsp sambar powder

In a pan, burst the mustard seeds in hot oil on medium heat, and fry the onion in it until caramelised.
Add garam masala, curry powder and paneer to the above and cook on low heat for 5 minutes, stirring occasionally.
Add salt, the tomatoes and peas.
Mix well, cover and cook for 15 minutes on low to medium heat, then add 2 tbsp water and cook for a further 10 minutes.
Mix in the coriander and sambar powder, cook on low heat for a further 15 minutes.

Dian's Tomato Chutney
Serves 6

2 inches root ginger or 1 tbsp ground ginger powder
1 tsp coriander seeds
1 tsp cumin seeds
1 tsp fenugreek seeds
1 ½ large green chillies slit in half
2 bay leaves
2 tsp brown sugar
1 tsp salt
2 tbsp oil
½ tsp asafoetida
850g fresh tomatoes in 1/8ths
2 tsp brown sugar

Grind ginger to a paste.
Heat oil in a pan, add the coriander, cumin and fenugreek seeds together with the asafoetida and cook on full heat until the cumin seeds turn brown.

Then add the ginger and cook for another minute.

Add chillies, tomatoes, salt and bay leaves and continue the cooking on full heat for 3 minutes stirring continuously.
Cover and reduce heat to low for 15 minutes.

Remove lid, increase heat to medium, add sugar, fish out the chillies and dispose of them and cook the mixture for another 15 minutes.

Leave to stand for at least 10 minutes before it is served.

Aubergine with coconut

Serves 8

For stage 1
2 large aubergines cut to ½ inch slices
2 dsp chilli powder
1 tsp spoon turmeric
1 tsp salt
50 ml water

For stage 2
2 medium onions coarsely chopped
100g creamed coconut, grated
6 cloves of garlic cut into chunks
4 medium sized green chillies slit half way
10 tbsp oil
1 tbsp garam masala
2 inches root ginger, cut to matchstick size
12 curry leaves
1 dessert spoon turmeric
550 ml boiling water

Stage 1
Mix the chilli powder, turmeric and salt into a paste with 50 ml water and smear a thin coating onto both sides of the aubergine slices.
Heat 8 tbsp of oil on high heat in a pan and fry the aubergine for two minutes each side until tender.
Remove from the heat and place on absorbent kitchen roll.

Stage two.

Add 400 ml of boiling water to the coconut.

Heat 2 tbsp oil in a pan and fry the onion until translucent, then add the ginger, garlic and chilli and fry for 3 or 4 minutes.

Add 1 teaspoon turmeric and the garam masala and continue to fry while stirring.

Add another 150 ml of water, reduce heat to medium and cover with a lid.

Cook for 5 minutes then add the coconut and the curry leaves, bring to the boil and cook the sauce for another 5 minutes.

Pre-heat the oven to 180°C.

Place the aubergine into a large flat ceramic dish and cover with the sauce.

Put in the oven and cook for 15 minutes, then lower the heat to 160^0 C for ten minutes.

RICE

Rice with peas
Serves 6.

200g rice
3 elaichi (cardamom) pods
2x 1" sticks cinnamon
2 cloves.
3 bay leaves
100g frozen peas
Oil
½ tsp salt

Rinse the rice and soak in water for about 10 minutes.
Then drain the water.
Heat 1 tablespoon of oil in a saucepan.
Add cardamom, cinnamon, cloves and bay leaves to the pan.
Cook for one minute.
Add the rice and salt.
Reduce heat and add 2 cups of boiling water. Cover with a tight lid and cook on low heat for 10 minutes.
Add the peas; cook on low heat for another 10 minutes.

Vegetable Pilav

Serves 12

250g fine green beans cut to 1 inch lengths
200g carrots cut to 1 inch cubes
100g fresh peas
3 cups rice (550g)
1½ tbsp pure butter ghee
1 tbsp oil
3 tbsp chopped coriander leaves
2 tbsp chopped mint
1 ½ tbsp garlic-ginger paste
5 cardamom pods
1 inch cinnamon stick, quartered
4 cloves
3 green chillies sliced lengthwise
6 cups water
2 cubes chicken or vegetable stock
1 onion, coarsely chopped

Soak the rice for 10 minutes. Drain the water off.
Set heat to a low – medium level.
Heat oil and ghee in a saucepan and add the onion, cinnamon,
cardamom pods \and cloves. Cook until the onion is translucent.
Then add the ginger-garlic paste.
Fry for one minute stirring continuously.
Now add the peas, carrots, beans, chillies, coriander leaves,
mint and salt to suit personal taste.
Dissolve stock cubes in 5 ½ to 6cups of hot water – add to the
pan and bring to the boil.
Mix the rice with the other ingredients.
Bring the pan to the boil, then reduce heat to medium, and cook
until the water reduces to nil.
*(The volume of water needed will vary with the type of rice used.
Use of personal judgement is essential)*

Kichdi

Serves 6

75g toor dhal (a cream coloured lentil)
100g mung dhal Yellow (yellow lentil without its skin)
175g rice
1 tbsp oil
1 ½ tsp cumin seeds
5 bay leaves
1" cinnamon stick
5 whole cloves
1 vegetable stock cube
1 tbsp ghee
6 black peppercorns
½ tsp salt

Dissolve the stock cube in 1 cup of boiling water.
Soak the dhal for 2 hours, rinse and drain
Rinse the rice.
Heat the oil and ghee in a deep saucepan. Add cumin seeds, cloves and peppercorns and fry until the cumin turns brown, then add the bay leaves and dhal.
Cook on high heat for one minute then reduce heat to medium, stirring continuously for 5 minutes.
Add the stock, cover and cook for 3 minutes.
Add the rice, salt and one more cup of water and cook on low to medium heat for 30 minutes.
Check after 15 minutes and if all the water has been used up, add another half cup.
Turn off heat and allow it to stand for 10 minutes.

Spinach Dhal
Serves 6

150g split mung dhal or split red lentils
½ tsp turmeric
250g fresh spinach
1 medium onion, finely chopped
2 medium green chillies slit in half, lengthwise
1 tsp mustard seeds
1 ½ tsp garam masala
1 tbsp tomato puree
1 tbsp oil
2 tsp ginger-garlic paste
½ tsp salt

Soak the dhal for half an hour, wash and cook in half a pint of water with the turmeric until the lentils are soft.
Heat oil in a pan and burst the mustard seeds.
Add the onion and fry until caramelised.
Add the ginger-garlic paste and reduce heat to medium.
Add the garam masala, chilli, tomato puree and the spinach and stir.
Add 2 tbsp of water, cover and cook for 5 minutes.
Add the dhal and salt and cook for another 2 minutes.
Serve with a garnish of coriander leaves.

SWEETS

Vermicelll Payasam

Serves 6

70g vermicelli
4 cardamom pods
1½ pints milk
2 heaped tablespoons sugar
16g butter
A few raisins and cashew nuts

Preheat oven to 200°C.
Place the vermicelli on a baking tray and cook in the oven for 3 minutes.
Split the cardamom pods open and put in a large bowl with the milk.
To this add the vermicelli and microwave on high power for 6 minutes.
Add the sugar and microwave full power for another 2 minutes.
Melt the butter in a small frying pan and fry the cashew nuts and raisins for 1 minute.
Mix it in with the payasam.
This may be served warm or cold.

Shrikand

Serves 6

¼ tsp saffron
2 x 500g natural Greek style yoghurt
90g caster sugar
8 cardamom pods (only the seeds are needed)
¼ tsp ground nutmeg
Tinned mandarin oranges
Chopped pistachio nuts.

Strain the yoghurt through muslin overnight.
Soak the saffron in 1 tbsp hot water and stand for at least half an hour.
Blend in the sugar with the yoghurt using a fork.
Crush cardamom seeds and add this together with the ground nutmeg to the sweetened yoghurt.
Finally, strain the liquid from the saffron using a tea strainer.
Blend this liquid into the yoghurt.

A serving suggestion
Place mandarin oranges in the bottom of a tall glass/a large glass bowl, then put in the above mixture, then a sprinkling of pistachio nuts on top.

Mango Fool

Serves 6

2 tbsp fresh milk
140 to 150ml evaporated milk
¼ tsp saffron (optional)
2 tbsp fine semolina powder
450g tin of mango pulp
2 tbsp ground almond powder
3 tbsp sugar
1 tsp cardamom powder
250g fromage frais
Tinned mango/tinned lychees/tinned mandarin orange segments

Warm the fresh milk and add the saffron.
Set to one side for half an hour.

Heat the evaporated milk in a saucepan and when almost to the boil, remove from the heat and add the semolina and stir rapidly until smooth.
Add the ground almonds, cardamom, sugar, mango pulp and the saffron milk. Chill for 2 to 3 hours.

Finally, mix in the fromage frais.
Garnish with slices of mango, tinned lychees or tinned mandarin orange segments.

Pancake with coconut filling

Serves 4

80g frozen coconut shreds
40 cardamom seeds, coarsely crushed
3 tbsp sugar
1 egg
About 300ml milk
100g flour
A pinch of salt

Mix the crushed cardamom seeds, the coconut and sugar.
Set it aside.

Make a batter by mixing egg, milk, flour and salt.
Heat a flat frying pan and wipe around with a little oil. Make thin
pancakes and roll up with the coconut filling.
Serve with a drizzle of maple syrup.

Mango and pineapple dessert
Serves 6

1 dsp cornflower
100 ml milk
2 tbsp sugar
425g tinned mango pulp
150 ml crème fraiche
Pineapple slices, either fresh or tinned

Mix the milk and cornflower in a bowl.
Cook in the microwave on maximum power for 30 seconds then
mix in the sugar.
Heat this mixture for another minute in the microwave.
Mix in the mango pulp and put in the fridge to chill.
After at least half an hour, beat to a smooth consistency.
Mix in half a tub of crème fraiche.
Pour into a serving dish and add pineapple as a topping.

Carrot Halva

Serves 8

750g grated carrot
750 ml milk
1 tbsp ghee
2 tsp cardamom powder
3 tbsp sugar
1 x 400 g tin sweetened condensed milk
90g sultanas

Put the carrot into a saucepan with the milk and **bring to the boil** *stirring continuously.*
Reduce heat and add the condensed milk, sugar and cardamom powder.
Simmer until the carrot mixture is thick – this is likely to be about an hour – stirring occasionally.
Finally, add the sultanas and ghee.

Lightly oil a flan dish and transfer the mixture into it. Allow to cool before serving.